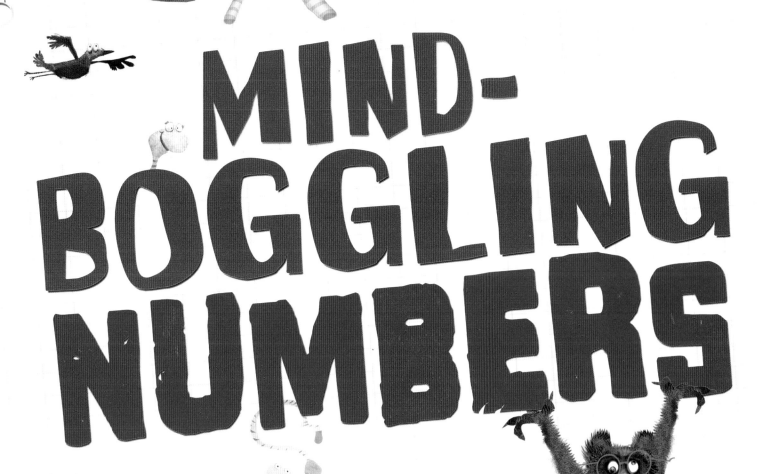

MIND-BOGGLING NUMBERS

Michael J. Rosen

illustrations by Julia Patton

M Millbrook Press/Minneapolis

To each young reader who might
be loving numbers...the way I
came to believing in words —MJR

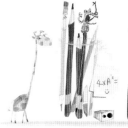   To my 4 x math-mad A's —JP

The publisher offers many thanks to Michael Mayers, math instructor at Illinois Central College, for his input on several particularly mind-boggling questions.

Text copyright © 2016 by Michael J. Rosen
Illustrations copyright © 2016 by Julia Patton

Millbrook Press
A division of Lerner Publishing Group, Inc.
241 First Avenue North
Minneapolis, MN 55401 USA

For reading levels and more information, look up this title at www.lernerbooks.com.

Design by Emily Harris
Main body text set in Bawdy Regular 12/18. Typeface provided by Chank.
The illustrations in this book were created with mind-boggling but happy mixed-media scribbles.

Library of Congress Cataloging-in-Publication Data

Names: Rosen, Michael J., 1954– author. | Patton, Julia, illustrator.
Title: Mind-boggling numbers / by Michael J. Rosen ; [illustrated by Julia Patton].
Description: Minneapolis : Millbrook Press, [2017] | Audience: Ages 7–11. | Audience: K to grade 3.
Identifiers: LCCN 2015043440 | ISBN 9781467734899 (lb : alk. paper) | ISBN 9781512411089 (eb pdf)
Subjects: LCSH: Mathematics—Juvenile literature. | Number concept—Juvenile literature.
Classification: LCC QA141.15 .R65 2017 | DDC 510—dc23

LC record available at http://lccn.loc.gov/2015043440

Manufactured in the United States of America
1-35569-15866-3/21/2016

Greetings from Ms. Mary Math!

Dear Readers,

I can't begin to calculate my delight with this book! It might be 94.6 percent! It might be close to a ton—2,000 pounds! It could even be 1,001 gallons of happiness.

Ever since I was young, whenever something involving arithmetic came along, friends and even grown-ups would say, "Oh, just give the math to Mary." Before long, my nickname had become Ms. Mary Math. And today, I'm *the* go-to wiz for mind-boggling math questions. So what's the story behind the book in your hands? It's a dozen doozies: story problems from all across the 2.3 billion acres that make up the United States.

To help you appreciate some of these amazing numbers, you'll find that I'm going to use *you* for a few comparisons. I know readers come in all shapes and sizes, but I'm going to pretend that you stand exactly 4 feet tall. That you weigh about 60 pounds. And that you can walk 1 mile in 20 minutes. These are all just averages, but you'll soon see how they can help us understand some truly tricky questions.

("What about metric conversions?" you ask. Or, at least, one of you faithful readers is bound to ask! You can find those at the end of the book.)

So let's get on with the math!

—MMM

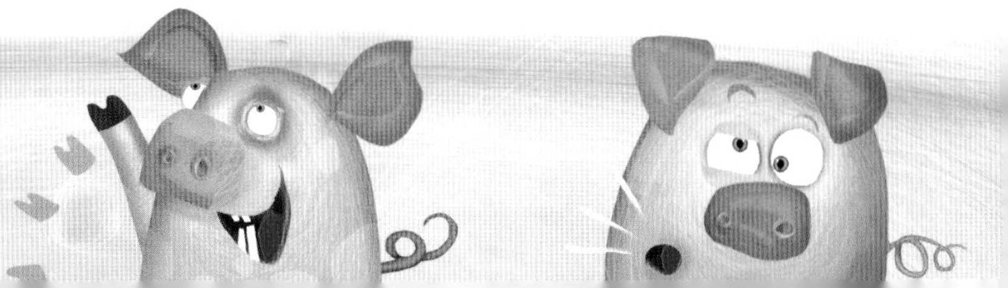

Dear Ms. Mary Math,

If I want a piggy bank that can hold a million pennies, how big does it need to be?

—Super Saver, Sandusky, OH

... piggy bank

Answer: A piggy bank for all those pennies . . . would be more like an elephanty-bank! Your million pennies add up to a total of $10,000.

Imagine a 1-gallon piggy bank—that's the size of a plastic milk jug. A single gallon holds 5,136 pennies. And that means you'll need 195 piggy banks to store your million pennies. So, really, you're looking at a piggy pen crammed with piggy banks.

And you're going to need some weight-lifting power. Those pennies will be heavy: 6,240 pounds! That's the weight of a *small* African elephant. Or twelve 500-pound Yorkshire pigs; they're one of the heftiest hogs around.

In short, your million pennies are nothing to snort about!

MiLk

ⓐ

ⓑ 1 Gallon Jug

ⓒ 5,136 pennies

Aaachooo!

oink oink

This
Way
up!

pennies

Heavy Load

Dear Ms. Mary Math,

I watched this cartoon in which these sparrows carried a blanket through the air. What if I were lying on top of that blanket? How many birds would I need to carry me?

—Sleepy in Anaheim, CA

 Tweet!

 Sparrow

wink

 ← 0.6 oz.

ⓑ

← 9 lb.

Hoot-Woot!

 Great Horned Owl

 ← 3 lb.

Answer: First of all, you'd better be on good terms with the local sparrow population. If you and your blanket weigh 60 pounds total, you'll need 1,600 house sparrows to lift you into the air. Each member of your flight crew can lift 0.6 ounces. That's the weight of 3 quarters.

And that's a huge flock of birds. Maybe you should consider a more powerful flier? How about the great horned owl. Weighing just 3 pounds, it can lift three times its weight: 9 pounds! So now, a mere 7 owls can serve as your flight crew.

Think about that. If you, at your 60 pounds, had such power, you could lift 180 pounds. That's like lifting a full-grown Great Dane!

180 lb.

Woof!

Great Dane

spLat!

7

Dear Ms. Mary Math,

Our school has a humongous swimming pool—like at the Olympics. If we wanted to turn it into the world's biggest lemonade stand, how many glasses would it hold?

—Sourpuss in Saugatuck, MI

Lemon

8 fl. oz. = 8 fl. oz.

Answer: Your pool, if it *is* Olympic-size, contains 660,000 gallons. It could hold just over 10.5 million "glasses" of lemonade, if each glass is 8 fluid ounces. That's the size of the milk carton you probably have in your cafeteria.

To get a sense of how much liquid that really is, let's look at what it would take to fill that pool. Imagine there are 600 kids in your school. On the first day of class, each and every student pours 98 cartons of lemonade into the empty pool. And every day, for the whole school year, everyone adds 98 more cartons.

On the last day of school—179 school days later—your pool will finally be full. When summer vacation arrives—when everyone is truly thirsty for some ice-cold lemonade—the pool will be filled . . . with warm, really old lemonade.

10.5 Million glasses

slurp

splash

Dear Ms. Mary Math,

All 20 kids in my class love blue whales. We sometimes see them in the bay that's exactly 1 mile from our school. I was wondering: If these gargantuan creatures lined up, just like we do at recess, how many blue whales would it take to reach our school?

—Krill Joy Was Here, Monterey, CA

Our School

1 Whale = 20 kids

Answer: For the moment, let's leave aside the question of how on earth you're going to get blue whales to line up. (Invite them to a krill buffet in your lunchroom?) Now, just how enormous are blue whales? The planet's largest existing creatures, they average 80 feet in length. If all 20 students in your class (remember, you're an average of 4 feet tall) lie head to foot on the floor, you would equal the length of a single blue whale.

Since your school is 1 mile away—that's 5,280 feet—we can divide those feet by 80, the length of one blue whale in feet. And there's your answer: 66 whales could line up between your school and the shoreline. In case you're wondering, to fill that same mile with 4-foot-tall students, lying head to foot, you'd need 1,320 kids. (That's 20 students to equal one 80-foot whale, multiplied by 66 whales.)

> Dear Ms. Mary Math,
>
> If I wanted to send a birthday card to everyone on the planet, how long would it take me to sign all those cards? I've got some free time this summer.
>
> —Grounded in Groveland, FL

Answer: That's a sweet thought. One problem: your task's impossible. Guess how long just signing each card with an *X* will take you? Your whole summer? A few years? Try a couple of *centuries!*

More than 7 billion people call Earth home. So let's imagine that you spend just 1 second on each card. To sign just 7 million cards, you'd need 7 million seconds. Convert those seconds into minutes, those minutes into hours, those hours into days, and it turns out you'll be signing for more than 81 days! That's probably your entire summer break. And yes, you'll have to skip sleeping, eating, biking, swimming, and anything else besides writing *X*s.

And then, you'd still have 6,993,000,000 more cards to sign! So if every 7 million cards takes just over 81 days, 7 billion cards will take about 222 years.

Maybe you could ask 10 friends to help. Then your 11-person team can knock out your planetary birthday wishes in a little more than 20 years!

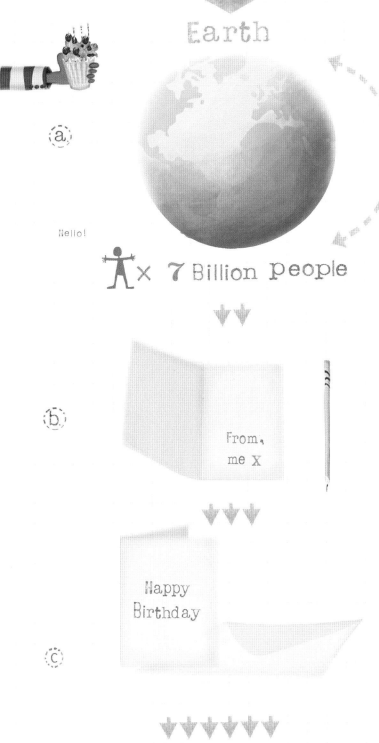

Hello!

Earth

ⓐ

$\stackrel{\text{\LARGE ♀}}{}$ × 7 Billion people

ⓑ From, me X

ⓒ Happy Birthday

$1 \times$ ♀ $= 7$ Billion cards $= 222$ Years

Dear Ms. Mary Math,

Our scout troop, the Muncie Moths, is visiting Yellowstone National Park because we heard grizzly bears love moths! There are 15 of us, and we're going to wear our super-cool moth costumes. I read that just one grizzly can eat 40,000 moths in a single day! In case we end up meeting a bear, we figured we should have a big moth meal ready so we can distract the bear and run. How long would it take us to collect 40,000 moths?

—Butterflies in My Tummy, Muncie, IN

Grizzly bear ⓐ

Gggrrr!

Eats 40,000 a day!

Muncie Moths scout ⓑ

ⓒ

1 Mile

Human = 3 Minutes, 43 seconds
Bear = 2 Minutes

Answer: It's true, grizzly bears need lots and lots of moths (and other food) to store up fat for winter. The bears dig the moths from the rocky mountainsides where they've burrowed. If each of you 15 scouts pluck 10 moths every minute, you'd have 150 moths. A mere mouthful to a bear! So to provide your grizzly with 40,000 moths, you'll need 267 minutes. That's well over 4 hours of digging! If your troop were a restaurant for bears, that grizzly will find your service *way too slow*!

And worse news: Grizzly bears aren't just huge—they're also hugely fast. Even if you sprinted as fast as the speediest human ever recorded, your time for 1 mile would be 3 minutes, 43 seconds. A grizzly runs nearly *twice* that fast! It can cover a mile in a mere 2 minutes!

I think the best strategy if you meet a bear would be this: accessorize your moth costumes with jet packs. Bears are no good at flying.

More than 4 Hours digging

dig dig dig

Yellowstone
National Park

Moths →

yummy

7 mph

30 mph

485 mph

Dear Ms. Mary Math,

My big brother just got his commercial pilot's license. We live 3 miles from my school. How long would it take me to get to school if he flies me there?

—Orville in Dayton, OH

Answer: Congratulations to your brother! A commercial airliner such as a Boeing 737 cruises at 485 miles per hour. If you're only 3 miles from school, the plane could zip you there in just over 22 seconds! That is, if you two were already airborne. But the real trouble is that your plane needs a runway that's at least 9,000 feet long for takeoff. And it needs a runway that's at least 7,500 feet for landing.

So if your driveway and the school did have the right size takeoff and landing strips—well, combined, those runways are longer than 3 miles! So the plane wouldn't even have its wheels off the ground before it would have to land.

But an even bigger problem: It's just not very fuel-efficient for an airplane that seats 149 people to fly a single passenger. To take off, a full 737 will burn almost 200 gallons of gas in a minute. A fairly fuel-efficient car can drive 30 miles using a single gallon of gas.

Better to save your brother's airliner for a vacation destination. The more efficient way to get to school? Take the bus—or better yet, ride your bike!

Dear Ms. Mary Math,

Is there anything more disgusting than worms? I know the answer: no! And my counselor says there are 1,000,000 worms in every acre of the meadows around our camp. So when we're out there eating lunch, how many worms are creepy-crawling under my 4-foot square picnic blanket?

—Squirming in Idaho

12 in.

12 in.

Answer: You won't like the upshot on these lowly critters. If there are 1 million worms in an acre, your particular lunch zone will contain about 370. Here's how you figure that.

For this problem, let's say that everyone's lunch box is a square—12 inches on each side. One acre that is an exact square would be 208.71 feet wide on all four sides. So about 43,560 lunch boxes would fit into that acre. That's about 209 rows with about 209 boxes in each row.

So if all million worms were distributed evenly underneath those 43,560 lunch boxes, you'd find a clew of 23 worms squiggling under each square. (Yep, a *clew* is the word for a group of worms.) Now it could be that worms have favorite hangouts, so your spot might have a few less . . . or it might have a few more. Your picnic blanket would cover 16 of those square feet, so multiply 16 by 23, and you get . . . 368 worms!

(If you want to upchuck your lunch now, we'll all look away.)

23 worms

1 acre

209 ft.

209 ft.

CAMP
ISOSCELES

LEG

OTHER LEG

VERTEX

ANGLE
LAKE

Dear Ms. Mary Math,

Numero, my Chihuahua, hates fleas. But fleas love him! I've heard that fleas are amazing jumpers. How high do I have to lift Numero to keep him free of these pesky biters?

—Freaked by Fleas, Memphis, TN

Fleas

If we could jump 100× our height

400 ft.

95 ft.

305 ft.

Answer: Fleas can jump about 100 times their body length. If you could jump 100 times your height, you'd be sailing 400 feet in the air. How high is that? You could easily hurdle the entire Statue of Liberty—with 95 feet to spare!

As it is, the most spectacular human jumpers can't rise more than 50 or 60 inches off the ground. That's not even a single body length into the air!

But a flea is only 0.06 inches long. Line up 17 fleas—and trust me, they don't like lining up—and you'll create a mere 1-inch itching machine. Still, each flea can only jump about 6 inches high. Therefore, Numero will enjoy a flea-free zone anywhere above your knees.

human with flea Power!

 (a)

 (b)

scritch scratch

Earth

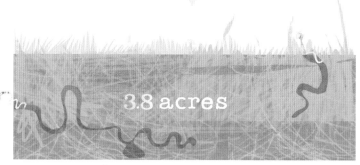

41.5 Million square miles

7 Billion people

3.8 acres

per human

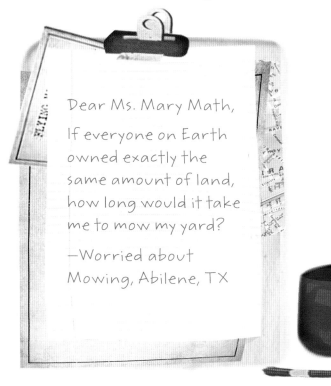

Dear Ms. Mary Math,

If everyone on Earth owned exactly the same amount of land, how long would it take me to mow my yard?

—Worried about Mowing, Abilene, TX

Answer: To answer this question, we need to figure out how much of the planet is habitable. Do *you* want to live high on a snow-covered mountain peak where only snowmen would enjoy the view? Do *you* want to live in the scorching-hot desert where only camels don't mind the heat? How about underwater? Didn't think so. Those uninhabitable regions remove about 16 million square miles from the real estate we can divvy up on Earth.

So we have 41.5 million relatively comfy square miles to split among Earth's 7 billion people. If you divide that habitable land evenly, we'd each own a property that contains 165,279 square feet.

So how big is that plot? You'd own about 3.8 acres. One acre, if it's a perfect square, is 208.7 feet on each side. Your mower, if its blade cuts a 2-foot-wide path, would need to make about 104 passes across your yard. That's 21,632 feet of mowing and walking. And it will take you 1.37 hours for 1 acre. *You own 3.8!* So multiply those hours by 3.8 acres . . . and you're looking at a little over 5 hours of mowing! (Hey, if you charged $10/hour, you'd make $50 cutting a neighbor's lawn!)

Woof!

BRrr BRrr BRrr

5 hours mowing @
$10.00 per hour = $50.00

putt putt putt

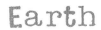

Earth

Dear Ms. Mary Math,

If there were a hiking trail between Earth and the moon, how long would it take me to walk the entire path?

—Lunatic in Los Cruces, NM

1 Mile = 20 mins.

(a)

(b) → 72 Miles = 1 day

Answer: Let's pretend there *is* a trail. Then the sign on Earth would read: **Moon 238,900 miles.**

For simplicity's sake, let's say that on this journey you don't break for meals, take a snooze, stop to soak your aching feet, or worry about oxygen, freezing temperatures, gravity, or any other atmospheric life-or-death details. That simplicity is impossible, but still, let's pretend you can hike a single mile in about 20 minutes. And you'll cover 72 miles in a day.

(c) → 26,280 Miles = 1 Year

Can you get to the moon in a year? Nope! You'll only have traveled 26,280 miles in that time.

So just how long will this expedition take? If you start your journey on the morning you turn 12, you'll spend about 9 years on your trek, celebrating your arrival on the moon shortly after your 21st birthday. Hey, you won't be a kid or even a teenager any longer! And by the time you're back on Earth, you'll be a real adult! (You *are* coming home, aren't you?) After those 9 years hiking back, you'll be ready to throw a belated 30th birthday party. Life is certainly a voyage!

(d)

9 total Years

moon

Dear Ms. Mary Math,

When it starts raining, if I get wet—so what!— I get wet. But what about tiny creatures, like mosquitoes? Can the raindrops squish them?

—Puddle Jumper in New Orleans, LA

Answer: It's so sweet that you worry about these irksome insects! But, in this case, you should find some needier critters to soak up that love.

Each mosquito weighs 2.5 milligrams. (Using the metric system for tiny weights is much easier than using the US customary system. A mosquito's weight barely tips registers on even a very tiny scale, so ounces aren't useful. It takes 400 skeeters to weigh 1 gram. That's what a paper clip weighs.)

Now, a typical raindrop weighs 50 times more than a mosquito: 125 milligrams. What if something 50 times heavier than you came splashing to the ground? Let's see, 50 times your weight of 60 pounds is 3,000 pounds! Imagine getting hit with a drop of water the weight of ten pianos!

Not only are mosquitoes incredibly light, but their bodies have a strong and flexible outer shell called an exoskeleton. So a skeeter can hitch a brief ride—it bodysurfs on a falling raindrop— and then breaks free, unharmed, before hitting the ground.

You, on the other hand, you . . . and those falling pianos of water: run for cover!

DO THE MATH!

1,000,000 Pennies (pages 4–5)

If the volume of each piggy bank is 1 gallon, about 5,136 pennies fit inside each one. (That's the average I found, plunking pennies into a 1-gallon milk jug.) By dividing 1 million pennies by the pennies that fit in one jug, you'll find that 195 piggy banks are needed to store them all. So 1,000,000 pennies ÷ 5,136 pennies per piggy bank = 195 piggy banks.

Now, why is your haul so heavy? One penny weighs a tenth of an ounce. So it takes 10 pennies together to make one ounce. And since there are 16 ounces in 1 pound, 160 pennies equal one pound. 5,136 pennies ÷ 160 pennies per pound = 32 pounds. So one piggy bank weighs 32 pounds. Now multiply that by the number of piggy banks, and you've got the total weight of your pennies. 32 pounds × 195 piggy banks = 6,240 pounds. African elephants weigh between 5,000 and 14,000 pounds.

How many Yorkshire piggies equal the weight of your million pennies? 6,240 pounds ÷ 500 pounds per pig = 12 pigs. That's 12 Yorkshire piggy banks.

Flying Blanket (pages 6–7)

Start like this: 60 pounds (your weight) × 16 (the number of ounces in a pound) = 960 ounces, your weight in ounces. Now 960 ounces ÷ 0.6 ounces (the weight each sparrow can lift) = 1,600, the number of sparrows in your flight crew.

Now if you went with the "owl force" instead: 60 pounds (your weight) ÷ 9 pounds (the amount of weight each owl can lift) = 6.667—let's say 7!—owls.

And the Great Dane you could lift if you had the owl's power? 60 pounds (your weight) x 3 = 180 pounds, about the weight of one of those hefty canines.

World's Biggest Lemonade Stand (pages 8–9)

An Olympic-size swimming pool is 164 feet long by 82 feet wide by 6.6 feet deep. Multiply those three numbers together to get the pool's volume, and you'll find that it can hold 88,757 cubic feet. One cubic foot holds 7.48 gallons, so 88,757 cubic feet × 7.48 gallons = 663,902, or about 660,000 gallons of water. One gallon is 128 fluid ounces. So 660,000 gallons × 128 fluid ounces = 84,480,000 total fluid ounces in the pool. One carton of lemonade is 1 cup, or 8 fluid ounces. Then 84,480,000 total fluid ounces ÷ 8 fluid ounces = 10,560,000 cartons needed to fill the pool.

So how do you figure it would take all year to fill the pool? 10,560,000 cartons ÷ 600 students = 17,600 cartons for each student to add. If your school year consists of 180 days, then: 17,600 cartons ÷ 180 days = 98 cartons to be added every school day. (The actual answer was 97.8 cartons, but I rounded up to 98 figuring a few drops might be left in each carton.)

Blue Whales (pages 10–11)

There's nothing fishy about these distance problems. 80 feet (the average length of a blue whale) ÷ 4 feet (the average student's height) = 20. So 20 students, lying down head to foot, are as long as a blue whale.

5,280 feet (the length of 1 mile) ÷ 80 feet (the blue whale's length) = 66. So 66 whales can line up, head to tail, from the shoreline to your school. Likewise, 5,280 feet (that same mile) ÷ 4 feet (the average student's height) = 1,320 kids lying down head to foot to create that mile. Or you could multiply 20 students per whale length × 66 whale lengths = 1,320 students.

Birthday Cards (pages 12–13)

Let's say you can sign a birthday card every second. Signing 7 million birthday cards will take you 7 million seconds. Let's convert seconds to days. 7,000,000 ÷ 60 seconds in a minute = 116,666.67 minutes. And then 116,666.67 minutes ÷ 60 minutes in an hour = 1,944.44 hours. Once more: 1,944.44 hours ÷ 24 hours in a day = 81.02 days needed to sign 7 million cards.

Since 7 billion is 1,000 times more than 7 million: 81.02 days × 1,000 = 81,020 days to sign 7 billion cards. How many years is that? 81,020 days ÷ 365 (the number of days in a year) = 221.97 years, which is just about 222 years.

And how long would each of the 11 birthday wishers sharing the task need to work? 222 years ÷ 11 = 20.18 years.

Moth-Munching Grizzly Bear (pages 14–15)

Assuming each scout can unearth 10 moths per minute, multiply that by the number of scouts to get your troop's moth-digging speed: 15 scouts × 10 moths each minute = 150 moths per minute. To find how much time the necessary 40,000 moths require, divide 40,000 by your troop's moths-per-minute rate: 40,000 moths ÷ 150 moths per minute = 267 minutes. 267 minutes ÷ 60 minutes in an hour = 4.45 hours of digging.

Flying to School (pages 16–17)

How long does it take the airliner to travel 1 mile if it's traveling 485 miles per hour? 485 miles × 5,280 feet in each mile = 2,560,800 feet per hour. Then 2,560,800 feet ÷ 60 minutes = 42,680 feet traveled in 1 minute. And once again: 42,680 feet ÷ 60 seconds in a minute = 711.3 feet traveled in 1 second. Since 1 mile is 5,280 feet: 5,280 ÷ 711.3 = 7.42 seconds for the time an airliner needs to cover 1 mile. You're 3 miles from school? That's 3 miles × 7.42 seconds = 22.3 seconds.

What's the trouble with the takeoff and landing distances? 9,000 feet to take off + 7,500 feet to land = 16,500 feet. The distance from the house to the school is 3 miles × 5,280 feet = 15,840 feet, which is shorter than the total length of the takeoff and landing distances.

Squirmy Worms (pages 18–19)

If an acre that's a perfect square is 208.71 feet on all sides, the space it contains—its area—in square feet can be found this way: 208.71 feet × 208.71 feet = 43,560 square feet. In other words, 1 acre contains 43,560 squares that are 1-foot on each side.

Earthworm populations depend on soil type, season, species, and available food, but 1 million worms in 1 acre represents a pretty healthy soil. 1,000,000 worms ÷ 43,560 lunch boxes (or square feet) = 23 worms for each 1-foot-square area. How many one-foot squares are in your 4-foot-square blanket? That's 4 feet × 4 feet = 16 square feet. So 23 worms × 16 square feet = 368 worms.

Pesky Fleas (pages 20–21)

If you could jump 100 times your 4-foot height that would be: 100 × 4 feet = 400 feet in the air. The Statue of Liberty is about 305 feet, from the base to the tip of the torch. You'd jump over the statue easily—with 95 feet of clearance.

A flea's length is 0.06 inches, so 17 fleas would fit in a 1-inch line (1 inch ÷ 0.06 inches = 16.67, or about 17 fleas). If it's jumping 100 times its body length, that's simply 100 × 0.06 = 6 inches.

Lots of Lawn to Mow (pages 22–23)

41,500,000 square miles ÷ 7,000,000,000 people on Earth = 0.00592857143 square miles for each inhabitant. Your 0.00592857143 square miles × 27,878,400 (the number of square feet in a square mile = 165,279 square feet of land in your yard. If 1 acre contains 43,560 square feet, then 165,279 square feet ÷ 43,560 square feet = 3.8 acres.

Think of each acre as a perfect square. Each side is about 208 feet long. So with your 2-feet-wide blade, you'd mow two 1-foot-wide rows at once. 208 feet ÷ 2 = 104 mowing rows. For 1 acre, 104 passes × 208 feet in a row = a walking/mowing distance of 21,632 feet. As mentioned before, you can probably walk 1 mile (which is 5,280 feet) in 20 minutes. 5,280 × 3 = 15,840 feet that you can walk in an hour. Your mowing distance of 21,632 feet ÷ 15,840 feet in an hour = 1.37 hours. Good job!

Oh, wait, you have 3.8 acres! So you're not just making 104 passes, but 3.8 × 104 = 395 passes. And then 395 rows × 208 feet in each row = 82,160 total feet you'll walk. Those 82,160 feet ÷ 15,840 feet you can walk in an hour = 5.18 hours. That's about 5 hours of mowing. And 5 hours × $10 per hour = $50.

Moon Walking (pages 24–25)

If you can walk 1 mile in 20 minutes, you can walk 3 miles in 60 minutes (that's 1 hour). Then 3 miles × 24 hours in a day = 72 miles traveled in 24 hours. To determine a year of walking, 72 miles per day × 365 days in a year = 26,280 miles.

The average distance from Earth to the moon, 238,900 miles ÷ 26,280 miles (the distance traveled in 1 year) = 9.09. So it'll take just over 9 years for that journey through space. If you began at age 12, 12 years + just over 9 years = 21 years—after your 21st birthday. After your return trip, you'll be 21 years + 9 years = 30 years old.

Soaking Mosquitoes (pages 26–27)

To see how many mosquitoes would weigh 1 gram (which is 1,000 milligrams): 1,000 milligrams ÷ 2.5 mg (1 bug's weight) = 400 mosquitoes.

One ounce is 28,349.5 milligrams. To find out how many mosquitoes are needed to equal 1 ounce: 28,349.5 milligrams ÷ 2.5 mg (1 bug's weight) = 11,340 mosquitoes.

A typical raindrop weighs 125 milligrams. 125 milligrams ÷ 2.5 milligrams = 50. So a raindrop is 50 times the weight of a mosquito. If you're a 60-pound kid, 50 times your body weight is 60 pounds × 50 = 3,000 pounds! Still need help picturing that? A small upright piano (like the one pictured) weighs about 300 pounds. 3,000 pounds ÷ 300 pounds = 10 pianos!

METRIC CONVERSIONS

MASS [WEIGHT]

US	Metric
0.1 ounces	2.84 grams
0.6 ounces	17 grams
1 ounce (= 28,349.5 milligrams)	28.35 grams
1 pound (= 16 ounces)	0.45 kilograms
3 pounds	1.36 kilograms
9 pounds	4.08 kilograms
32 pounds	14.5 kilograms
60 pounds (= 960 ounces)	27.22 kilograms
180 pounds	81.65 kilograms
300 pounds	136.1 kilograms
500 pounds	227 kilograms
2,000 pounds	907.2 kilograms
3,000 pounds	1,361 kilograms
5,000 pounds	2,268 kilograms
6,240 pounds	2,830 kilograms
14,000 pounds	6,350 kilograms
1 ton	907.2 kilograms

VOLUME

US	Metric
8 fluid ounces (= 1 cup)	236.6 milliliters (= .24 liters)
1 gallon (= 128 fluid ounces)	3.79 liters
7.48 gallons (1 cubic foot)	28.31 liters
12 gallons	45.42 liters
200 gallons	757 liters
1,001 gallons	3,789 liters
660,000 gallons (= 84,480,000 fluid ounces)	2,498,000 liters (= 2,498 cubic meters)
88,757 cubic feet	2,513 cubic meters

LENGTH

US	Metric
0.06 inches	1.52 milimeters
1 inch	2.54 centimeters
6 inches	15.24 centimeters
12 inches (= 1 foot)	30.48 centimeters
50 inches	127 centimeters
60 inches	152.4 centimeters
2 feet	60.96 centimeters
4 feet	1.22 meters
6.6 feet	2.01 meters
80 feet	24.38 meters
82 feet	25 meters
95 feet	29 meters
164 feet	50 meters
208 feet	63.4 meters
208.7 feet	63.61 meters
305 feet	93 meters
400 feet	122 meters
5,280 feet (1 mile)	1.61 kilometers
7,500 feet	2.29 kilometers
9,000 feet	2.74 kilometers
15,840 feet	4.83 kilometers
16,500 feet	5.03 kilometers
21,632 feet	6.59 kilometers
82,160 feet	25.04 kilometers
3 miles	4.83 kilometers
6,000 miles	9,656 kilometers
30 miles	48.28 kilometers
72 miles	116 kilometers
26,280 miles	42,290 kilometers
238,900 miles	384,500 kilometers

AREA

US	Metric
1 square foot	0.09 square meters
4 square feet	0.37 square meters
16 square feet	1.49 square meters
43,560 square feet	4,047 square meters
165,279 square feet	15,360 square meters
0.00592857143 square miles	15,360 square meters
27,878,400 square feet (= 1 square mile)	2.59 square kilometers
16 million square miles	41,440,000 square kilometers
41.5 million square miles	107,500,000 square kilometers
1 acre	4,047 square meters
3.8 acres	15,380 square meters
2.3 billion acres	9,308,000 square kilometers

SPEED

US	Metric
711.3 feet per second (= 42,680 feet per minute)	216.8 meters per second
10 miles per hour	16.09 kilometers per hour
30 miles per hour	48.28 kilometers per hour
485 miles per hour (= 2,560,800 feet per hour) (= 42,680 feet per minute)	780.5 kilometers per hour (= 13,008.86 meters per minute)

KEY CONCEPTS

area: This is a measurement of the size of a surface. To calculate the area of a rectangle, multiply the width by the length. In mathematical terms, that's $A = w \times l$. Measurements of area are expressed in square units, such as square feet (ft^2), square miles (mi^2), or square kilometers (km^2). This website provides formulas for calculating the areas of other shapes: http://www.coolmath.com/reference/areas.

speed: This is a measurement of how fast an object is traveling. To calculate speed, divide the distance traveled by the time it takes to travel that distance. In mathematical terms, that's $S = d \div t$. Measurements of speed are expressed in units of length per period of time, such as miles per hour (mph) or meters per second (m/s).

volume: This is a measurement of the amount of space an object takes up or how much a certain container can hold. To calculate the volume of a rectangular cube, multiply the length by the width by the height. In mathematical terms, that's $V = w \times l \times h$. Measurements of volume are expressed in cubic units, such as cubic feet (ft^3) or, for liquid volume, units such as gallons or liters. This website provides formulas for calculating the volume of other shapes: http://www.basic-mathematics.com/volume-formulas.html.

FOR FURTHER READING

BOOKS

Ash, Russell. *Factastic Book of Comparisons*. New York: DK, 1999.
——. *Incredible Comparisons*. New York: DK Children, 1996.
Both books present insightful graphs, charts, and illustration to reveal the weight, size, height, speed, or other physical properties of many objects by showing equivalents: for instance, the Great Pyramid weighs as much as 156 Statues of Liberty.

Rosen, Michael J. *The 60-Second Encyclopedia*. New York: Workman, 2005.
A 320-page gathering of a minute's worth of almost everything. Categories range from beats and spins to things manufactured and foods consumed, all measured in 60-second increments. The book comes with a minute-glass and many activities that kids can do.

Schwartz, David M. *How Much Is a Million?* New York: Lothrop, Lee & Shepard Books, 1985.
Schwartz's book—as well as two others in the series, *If You Made a Million*, and *Millions to Measure*—features Marvelissimo the Mathematical Magician. With the help of friends and pets, he shows vast quantities and confusing numerical concepts in playful, far-fetched visualizations. For example, a bowl large enough to fit a million goldfish could hold a 60-foot whale.

WEBSITES

The Math Forum @ Drexel
http://www.mathforum.org/students/
Geared toward various grade levels, Drexel University's multifaceted site features activities, tools, tricks, challenges, and references all pertaining to math. Of particular appeal is the wonderful question-and-answer forum, "Ask Dr. Math."

The Scale of the Universe
http://www.htwins.net/scale/
This is the first "Scale of the Universe" project, which allows a visitor to navigate from the smallest subatomic particulars to living creatures to structures in the built environment to the grandest masses of the solar system. Created by Carey and Michael Huang, this site hosts a second video on scale, as well as many other interactive math and science videos.